Ernie's Joke Book

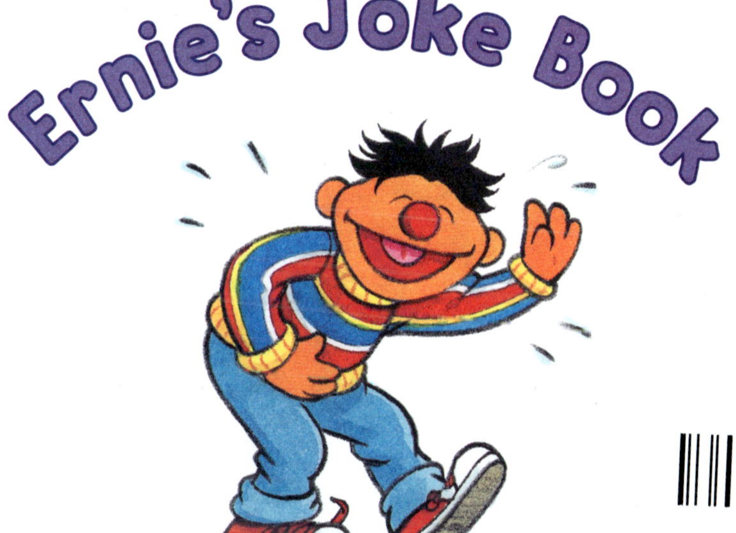

By Sarah Albee

Illustrated by Joe Mathieu

Featuring Jim Henson's Sesame Street Muppets

A Random House PICTUREBACK® Shape Book

 Published in the United States by Random House, Inc., New York, and simultaneously in Canada by Random House of Canada Limited, Toronto, in conjunction with Sesame Workshop. Sesame Street, Sesame Workshop, and their logos are trademarks and service marks of Sesame Workshop.

Library of Congress Catalog Card Number: 00-103519 ISBN 0-375-81155-9

www.randomhouse.com/kids/sesame

www.sesamestreet.com

Printed in the United States of America January 2001 10 9 8 7 6 5 4 3 2 1

PICTUREBACK, RANDOM HOUSE, and the Random House colophon are registered trademarks of Random House, Inc.

Hey, Ernie. I have the funniest joke for you. Here it is: Why did the chicken cross the road?
Give up, Ernie? The answer is: To get to the other side! Get it?
REALLY BORING JOKES THAT EVERYONE HAS HEARD ALREADY

That's a really funny joke, Bert! And guess what? I have a whole book here that's full of <u>more</u> funny jokes!

Why did the chicken cross the playground?

To get to the other slide.

Why did the cow cross the road?

To get to the udder side.

Waiter! This soup tastes funny!
Well, then why are you not laughing, sir?

What do you call a penguin in the desert?

Lost.

What is a bird's favorite TV show?

The feather forecast.

How do you put a pizza back together?

With tomato paste.

Knock, knock.
Who's there?
Cows go.
Cows go who?

Cows don't go *who,* silly. They go *moo*.

Three big monsters were standing under one tiny umbrella. Why didn't any of them get wet?

It wasn't raining.

What runs but never walks?

Water.

How do skunks make telephone calls?

On their smellular phones.

Knock, knock.

Who's there?

Atch.

Atch who?

Uh-oh. Sounds like you're coming down with a cold.

What do you get when you cross a gorilla and a parrot?

"Polly wants a cracker—NOW."

Where do sheep get their wool cut?

At the baa-baa shop!

What animal should you never play cards with?
Hey! Something's fishy about this Go Fish game!
A cheetah.

Why did the orange go to the doctor?

It wasn't peeling well.

If a monster has five balls in one hand and four in the other, what does he have?

Very large hands.

Why did the leopard lose at hide and seek?

It was spotted.

Where do cows go for fun?

To the mooooooooovies.

Okay, Bert, how about this one? What do you call a bull that's sleeping?
A bulldozer!
That's a funny one, Ernie! Now I have one! What did one polar bear say to the other polar bear?
Have an ice day!

Wow, Bert! That really is a funny joke!
Thanks, Ernie.

FULL THROTTLE

INDY CARS

BY THOMAS K. ADAMSON

EPIC

BELLWETHER MEDIA • MINNEAPOLIS, MN

EPIC BOOKS are no ordinary books. They burst with intense action, high-speed heroics, and shadows of the unknown. Are you ready for an Epic adventure?

This edition first published in 2019 by Bellwether Media, Inc.

Library of Congress Cataloging-in-Publication Data

Names: Adamson, Thomas K., 1970- author.
Title: Indy Cars / by Thomas K. Adamson.
Description: Minneapolis, MN : Bellwether Media, Inc., [2019] | Series: Epic. Full Throttle | Audience: Ages 7-12. | Audience: Grades 2 to 7. | Includes bibliographical references and index.
Identifiers: LCCN 2018032002 (print) | LCCN 2018033012 (ebook) | ISBN 9781618916570 (ebook) | ISBN 9781626179325 (hardcover : alk. paper)
Subjects: LCSH: Indy cars–Juvenile literature. | Automobiles, Racing–Juvenile literature.
Classification: LCC TL236 (ebook) | LCC TL236 .A327 2019 (print) | DDC 629.228/5-dc23
LC record available at https://lccn.loc.gov/2018032002

Editor: Christina Leaf   Designer: Jeffrey Kollock

Printed in the United States of America, North Mankato, MN

TABLE OF CONTENTS

A DARING MOVE

Indy cars zip around the track. They dart back and forth as they try to pass. The driver in fourth place zooms forward to move into second place. But the leader blocks him!

Two laps later, he moves to the outside on a turn. He shoots in front of the lead car.

New leader! He pulls away and wins the race!

WHAT ARE INDY CARS?

Indy cars are **open-wheel** race cars. They scream around road courses and oval racetracks. Some courses use city streets as part of the racetrack.

The most famous track is the Indianapolis Motor Speedway. It hosts the Indianapolis 500!

Indy cars are light, **agile** racers. They can speed up and turn quickly.

Indy cars are **aerodynamic**.
They are built to cut easily through the air.
The drivers sit low in the center of the car.

THE HISTORY OF INDY CARS

Indianapolis had many car factories in the early 1900s. A large, paved test track was needed to try new car designs.

Indianapolis 500, 1913

THE INDY NAME

"Indy" is short for "Indianapolis." The cars are named after the test track.

Such a track also worked for racing. These races showed off the strengths of the factories' cars.

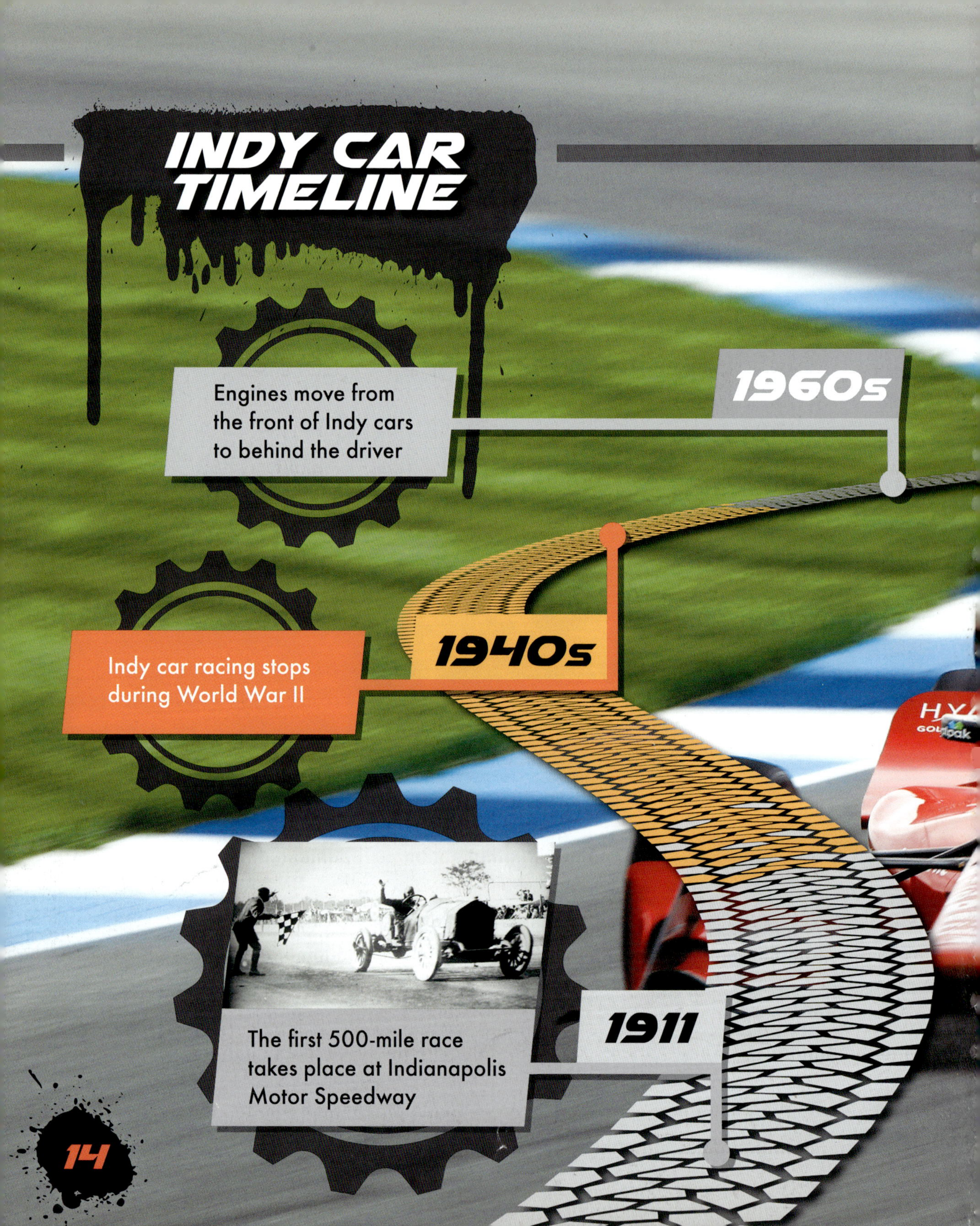
INDY CAR TIMELINE
1960s
Engines move from the front of Indy cars to behind the driver
1940s
Indy car racing stops during World War II
1911
The first 500-mile race takes place at Indianapolis Motor Speedway

Over time, Indy car designs changed with new **technology**. Racing became faster and more exciting. Indy car technology also improved regular cars' safety and performance!

INDY CAR PARTS

The **chassis** is the body of an Indy car. The driver sits in an open **cockpit**. A **roll hoop** sticks up behind the driver's head. It protects the driver in case of a rollover.

TUB RACING

The chassis is also called the tub.

WING INNOVATION

A bolted-on rear wing was first used at the Indy 500 in 1972.

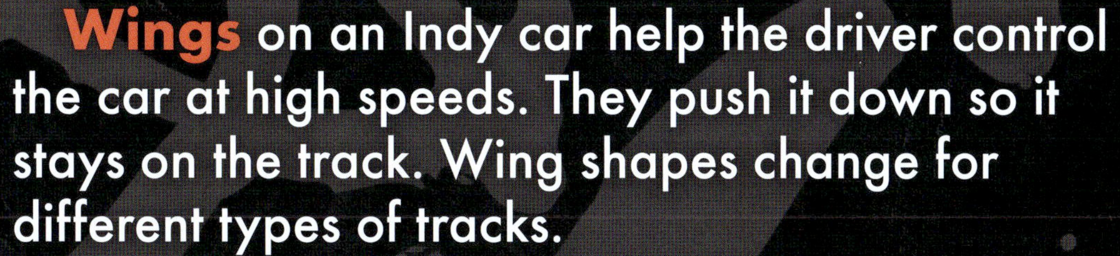

Wings on an Indy car help the driver control the car at high speeds. They push it down so it stays on the track. Wing shapes change for different types of tracks.

IDENTIFY AN INDY CAR

INDY CAR COMPETITIONS

Indy car drivers race for teams in the IndyCar Series. Each race has many laps. Races can be hundreds of miles long.

INDY SPEED

Indy cars reach the highest speeds during the Indianapolis 500. They can hit 235 miles (378 kilometers) per hour!

Drivers win points based on how they finish. Indy car races are high-speed action!

GLOSSARY

aerodynamic—designed to move through air quickly and easily

agile—able to move quickly and easily

chassis—the frame of an Indy car

cockpit—the place where the driver sits

open-wheel—a race car that has the wheels out in the open and not under the car's body

roll hoop—the part of an Indy car that protects the driver in a rollover

technology—the use of science and engineering to do practical things

wings—parts of an Indy car that use aerodynamics to push down on the car to give it more control

TO LEARN MORE

AT THE LIBRARY

Fishman, Jon M. *Cool Indy Cars.* Minneapolis, Minn.: Lerner Publications, 2019.

Lanier, Wendy Hinote. *Indy Cars.* Lake Elmo, Minn.: Focus Readers, 2017.

Workman, Chris. *The Spectacle: Celebrating the History of the Indianapolis 500.* Huntersville, N.C.: Apex Legends, 2017.

ON THE WEB

FACTSURFER

Factsurfer.com gives you a safe, fun way to find more information.

1. Go to www.factsurfer.com.

2. Enter "Indy cars" into the search box.

3. Click the "Surf" button and select your book cover to see a list of related web sites.

INDEX

The images in this book are reproduced through the courtesy of: Honda Media Center, front cover, pp. 14-15, 15 (2018), 16-17, 19 (engine); Digital First Media/ Getty Images, pp. 4-5; Brian Cleary/ Getty Images, pp. 6, 7; Action Sports Photography, pp. 8-9, 20-21; tpsdave/ Wikipedia, p. 9; Jon Nicholls Photography, pp. 10, 18-19; Dave Reginek/ Getty Images, p. 11; Bain News Service/ Library of Congress, pp. 12, 14 (1911); RacingOne/ Getty Images, pp. 12-13; David Taylor/ Getty Images, p. 15 (1996); Darren Brode, p. 19; MACH Photos, p. 20.